The Silent Years

The Silent Years

Lance Lambert

LANCE LAMBERT MINISTRIES

Richmond, VA

ISBN 978-1-68389-098-0
www.lancelambert.org

Contents

Preface

Have you ever thought of what happened in the four hundred years between Malachi in the Old Testament and Matthew in the New Testament? It seems as if God was silent during those years until John the Baptist was raised up announcing the arrival of the Messiah's first coming. But even though God did not speak with Scriptures during those years there He was working and preparing the way for the arrival of Immanuel.

In this volume Lance Lambert seeks to show what God was doing behind the scenes during this silent period between the two testaments of Scripture. May the Lord use this account of the silent years to encourage His people in this current time of preparation for His soon coming.

1.
Intertestamental Period–Part 1

The Four Hundred Silent Years

The period between the end of the Old Testament Canon and the beginning of the New Testament has been called "the four hundred silent years." They may indeed have been silent insofar as there was no great prophetic voice or any appearance of directly inspired Scripture. If, however, we were to think of divine activity, these four hundred years were anything but silent. Tremendous and far-reaching changes took place in every sphere of human life. Great world empires vanished and others appeared. The Jews were scattered throughout the inhabited earth, and wherever they went they gathered together for worship and study and became a testimony of the living God to the Gentiles. The Word of God, the very revelation of God Himself, was translated in its entirety into Greek, and thus millions became aware of something that before had been hidden.

The Promised Land itself was prepared, as were the nations—culturally, politically, and religiously—for the coming of the Messiah. The canon of the Old Testament was finally recognized as complete; it was the witness to the coming Saviour of the world. In view of all this, it is then of real importance that we should investigate this period.

The Gentile World Empires

Let us first look at the Gentile background. During this period three successive world empires operated: namely Persia, Greece, and Rome. And the course of these empires, as they touched the people and work of God, had been remarkably foretold in the book of Daniel. From each of these empires we can learn a tremendous amount. Let us take a look at their successive order.

Persia

On the whole, the Persian system of government was enlightened and humane. They had allowed the return of deported peoples to their own lands and the reconstruction of their lives under a limited form of home rule. The fact that the Persians were Zoroastrians, worshipping the one invisible God whom they believed was Spirit, and whose symbol was fire, meant that they felt a kinship with the Jews as with no other. They had, therefore, on the whole favoured the reconstruction of Jerusalem and the temple. Gradually, however, internal divisions and rebellion weakened them until they were finally swept away by Alexander the Great in 335 BC. Thus God used Persia for the fulfilling of His purpose—the rebuilding of the temple and the city, reinstitution of the priesthood and true worship, repopulation of the land, and the study of the Word of God. This was all in preparation for the coming Messiah.

Greece

In 334 BC Greece arose as another great world power. Greece already had a culture and civilization famed for its brilliance long before this. It was, however, Alexander the Great, one of the most remarkable men in world history, who led Greece into its greatest era, in an empire that extended from the Dardanelles to India. Its rise to supreme power began with Alexander's father, Philip of Macedon, when he had united Thrace, Macedonia, and Greece. He then started on an offensive to free Greek areas under Persian domination. He was assassinated in 236 BC and was succeeded by his twenty-year old son, Alexander. When he was only twenty-five, he conquered Persia and then went on from triumph to triumph until he headed the greatest empire of that day.

Alexander died in Babylon in 323 BC of fever at the age of thirty-one. Although his life was short, and the unity of his empire did not last long, he imposed upon the ancient world a cultural unity which was to last one thousand years. From then on Hellenism permeated every part of the old empire. Greek became the common and universal language, and the old Semitic languages fell slowly into a kind of disuse. Greek thought, customs and traditions were adopted everywhere. Upper class society became Hellenized. Great changes came in the fields of art, philosophy, and science, as well as religion. So Hellenized did the ancient world become, that to the true Jews all Gentiles were "Greeks"!![1]

Great cities arose like Alexandria—magnificent in its properties and architecture. Its seaport and harbour were unrivalled in antiquity; it became one of the greatest intellectual centres of the known world. Public libraries, zoos, gardens, and museums all added to its fame. It was here that Greek-speaking Jews, called Hellenist Jews, found their centre and it was from here that the Greek translation of the Hebrew Old Testament—Septuagint (LXX.)—was translated

Great Greek philosophers—Plato, Aristotle, Socrates, Epicurus, Zeno—all in some way prepared the Gentile world for Christ, the Messiah. Alongside all that was good and commendable in Hellenistic society, corruption, immorality, and a pursuit of pleasure developed which has become proverbial. It was during this period, toward the end, that one of the darkest and most sinister characters predicted in Daniel appeared. It was one of Jewry's darkest hours. That man was Antiochus IV Epiphanes, whose attempt to Hellenize the temple led to severe persecution. He became the arch type of antichrist. The trademark and legacy of Hellenism is humanist philosophy—everything begins with man and ends with man. Even the gods are human with all the failings of human beings. Everything is the projection of the human mind.

Greece's contribution to the coming of the Messiah was undoubtedly the cultural unity it created over a large area, and the liberalizing attitude and tendency of Greek thought and culture. However, it was supremely the Greek language which

1 see I Corinthians 1:22–24; Galatians 3:28; Colossians 3:11

became both in writing and in speech the means of the gospel reaching the whole empire.

Rome

In 66 BC the last great world empire rose to its zenith. For some centuries Rome's sun had been slowly rising. Under the able leadership of Pompey in the Eastern Mediterranean and Julius Caesar in the West, it came to its supreme power. Rome was different to all that preceded it in its democratic form of government, already known in individual Greek city-states. Its genius lay in the way it bound territory after territory to itself with bilateral agreements, giving much local independence, while taking on overall administrative and military responsibility. While in theory government was democratic, in practice it soon became autocratic with the Emperor being looked upon as divine. In fact, the army and its allegiance to Caesar became the central and definitive factor.

At its greatest point, the empire stretched from the Atlantic to the Euphrates, from the British Isles to African deserts, the Nile cataracts and the Arabian Desert, leaving only Germany and Parthia remaining outside. The Roman Empire was divided by provinces responsible to the Roman Senate, and governed by a proconsul for a year; and imperial provinces responsible directly to the Emperor and governed by legates and procurators appointed by him.

Roman citizenship was something greatly sought after because of its privileges. Colonies, such as Philippi, were peopled by such citizens who were originally sent out from Rome. Other cities, such as Athens, were granted Roman citizenship. By these means

Rome insured itself against rebellion. Rome gave to the world justice, the rule of law, which has become the basis of all justice to this day. It created an administrative machine from Babylon to Scotland unequalled in world history, whilst its roads, public buildings, and works have become world famous.

Rome combined military might and strength with justice and public order. Its system of roads (many of which have lasted until today) gave to the empire a transport system never before known. The Roman army was divided into legions. Each legion numbered about ten thousand men. A legion was divided into ten cohorts of infantry, each numbering four hundred and eighty men. It also had a cavalry company and an artillery unit. Many times in the New Testament *centurions* are mentioned. They were officers who commanded a company of one hundred men.

The contribution of Rome to God's purpose was that at Christ's coming the world was strongly and harmoniously governed— law protected religions, the Roman network of roads was protected from brigands which meant that the Gospel could be speeded from Spain to Russia and from Babylon to Scotland.

The Jewish Background

In order to understand the Jewish background of the New Testament, we need to remember that Jewish life flowed into two distinct streams during the Intertestamental period. Both streams shared completely in all the fundamentals of the faith, but beyond that they differed greatly. Indeed, there was more than a little antipathy between them. One stream— the go ahead, open-minded, liberal stream—is called in the New

Testament *Hellenists*. The other one, which is the conservative, narrow and puritanical stream, is called *Hebrews*.

The Hellenists

Let's look at the Hellenists first. We find this term in a number of New Testament writings[2] and it was used of the Jews who were dispersed throughout the Gentile world outside of the Promised Land, from the Euphrates area and East; to Spain and France in the West (and even Germany); to Arabia, Egypt and Ethiopia in the South. We even know of a Jewish community and synagogue in KaiFeng in China from the inscription made in 1488 AD which speaks of a synagogue in 1166 AD. Another says that the Jewish faith entered China in 3rd Century AD. This dispersion began probably as early as Solomon's reign in the establishment of commercial outposts in different Gentile centres. Certainly its greater development came through the deportation of Israel's upper classes by Assyria in 728 BC and again at the fall of Judah in 586 BC by Babylon, and the fleeing of others at a later time to Egypt. Thus, its real rise can be traced originally to the judgment of God.[3]

The Jewish communities throughout Babylon, Asia Minor, and Egypt became well established and prosperous. Indeed there is evidence that they dominated much not only of business life but also professional life. These communities that had been cured of idolatry and were worshipping the living God were utterly distinctive in every way in their Gentile setting. When the

2 II John 7:35; James 1:1; I Peter 1:1 cf. Acts 2:5, 8–11. Note also Acts 6:1
3 Deuteronomy 28:26, 36, 64–65

Persians came to power and permitted the return of the deported peoples, the majority of Jews remained. These became the basis of "The Diaspora" or "The Dispersion." They had adopted for the most part the customs and background of the surrounding Gentiles, and indeed some of their spirit; yet they remained essentially aloof.

It was with Alexander and the Greek era, and the universal adoption of Greek and their customs that these Jewish communities became Hellenized and were given the name *Hellenists* by the Jews in the homeland. Gradually, Jews settled further and further afield, continually increasing by fresh emigration from the homeland, and multiplying wherever they settled. In the 4th century AD Philo numbered the Jews in Egypt as one million. Philo says of Cyrene: "This people has made its way into every city, and it is not easy to find a place in the habitable world which has not received this nation, in which its power has not been felt." As early as 139 BC there was an expulsion order against the Jews in Rome.

Alexandria became the natural centre for all the Hellenists. Jews occupied two of the five city quarters. Its magnificent synagogue was famous. The export of grain was in Jewish hands, Egypt being the granary of the known world. Sometime during the 2nd century BC they produced the Septuagint (LXX Version.), perhaps the greatest single contribution to the coming of Christ by the Hellenists. Much other literature was produced in Alexandria, which showed the very real influence of Greek thought upon Jewish faith, e.g. "Wisdom of Solomon." Philo, the great Jewish philosopher, found in Greek philosophy the real meaning of the Jewish Scriptures.

These communities, whose life centred in the synagogue, had a considerable influence. The Hellenists were not narrow, cautious and puritanical like the Hebrews. They appeared to take the best of Greek culture and thought while remaining altogether different. They had an ethical, moral code, a family life, an understanding of God that was by far superior to anything in the Gentile world. For whilst the Hellenists imbibed much of the Greek spirit and introduced many innovations to Jewish life, they remained absolutely loyal to the Scriptures—the Law, the coming Messiah, the Sabbath, Jerusalem, the temple sacrifice and worship.

2.
Intertestamental Period–Part 2

All good Hellenist Jews sent the yearly half shekel, the temple tax, and sought to make pilgrimages to the temple at the great feasts. In fact, many wanted to die and be buried in Jerusalem, Thus, there was always a large Hellenist colony there. The more restrictive practices and limitations they put aside, tending to see and emphasize the inner and essential meaning of the faith. And it was this combination of Greek thought and true living faith which appealed to many Gentiles.

Moreover, the Hellenists had a far greater missionary spirit than the Hebrews (among whom it was well-nigh non-existent). Thus it was that in any synagogue of the Dispersion, from East of the Euphrates to Spain, Gentiles could hear the Word of God read and explained in their own language. They could listen to the worship of the one Living God, and they could hear of the coming Messiah and Deliverer. They could see in those people a kind of life and knowledge nowhere else to be found. So it came to be that all over the Roman Empire and beyond, large numbers of Gentile converts were attached to almost every synagogue. We come to know these Gentile converts in the New Testament.

There would have been those who had been admitted into the faith fully, with circumcision, baptism and sacrifice. These were allowed all the privileges of a Jew. There was also another class who were not circumcised yet they attended synagogue and believed. They were called "God fearers," "devout men or women" or "ones who worshipped God." There has been much discussion about these proselytes. Later, Jewry made a distinction between "Proselytes of Righteousness" who were full Jews, having been circumcised, baptized, and so forth, and "Proselytes of The Gate" who were those who believed but were not circumcised.

There has also been discussion about baptism as the mode or rite of admittance. It is not mentioned in the Old Testament, but there is more than a little evidence for it. What does seem clear is that by New Testament times there were many Gentiles who became full Jews, and many who accepted the faith but did not go the whole way. The influence of the Hellenists and others in the Dispersion on the New Testament cannot be minimized. Here is the evidence of God in history turning even judgment into good!

We can sum up its contribution thus: a universal view of things taking in Gentile as well as Jew, an understanding of the times and the essential meaning of the faith, the Scriptures appearing in Greek, and the necessary first step to the New Testament in Greek. No Hebrew would have countenanced such a step. In nearly every sizeable Gentile community in the Roman Empire and beyond, there was a Jewish synagogue with a large number of

Gentile converts. It was a centre of Biblical teaching among other activities. Thus there was a "spirit of preparation and anticipation" for the coming Messiah. It was to these centres that the first Messianic believers went. Most of the great believers in the early church were Hellenists—Stephen, Barnabas, Philip, Apollos, Timothy, Silvanus, Titus, Aquila and Priscilla. Paul was a Hebrew but brought up in Hellenistic Tarsus. It was among the Hellenists and the "God fearers" that the gospel made such headway into the purely Gentile world.

The Hebrews

"The Hebrews" by New Testament times had become a name for all the Aramaic and Hebrew speaking Jews in the Land. They were of decidedly nationalistic sympathies. "The Hebrews" covered all who adhered strictly and in a puritanical way to the faith.[1] They had resisted the influences of Greek thought and culture, and remained "Jewish Jewish!" They regarded Hellenism as second grade Judaism, a semi-heretical form of the faith. They looked upon the innovations of Hellenistic Jews with absolute horror as looseness and adaptation. To them it was the sign of grave apostasy. They felt that the true stream of divine life and light was with them. They were the true successors to the patriarchs and prophets, the true guardians of the Oracles of God.

---

1 Acts 6:1; II Corinthians 11:22; Philippians 3:5

The Three Parties in Israel

Among the people of God in the homeland there gradually developed over the four centuries three parties—the Pharisees, the Sadducees and the Essenes. These three are inseparably linked to the New Testament. Let us take a look at their respective profiles.

The Pharisees
The Pharisees were a party on the extreme right wing, which grew up after the return from Babylon. They felt the need, in the light of the tremendous inroads of Hellenism, to protect the pure and true faith. Originally, they were known as the *Chasidim*—the *Pious*. This broke into two wings—the small nationalistic political party called the *Zealots*[2] and the much larger, more popular party of the Pharisees, probably a nickname[3], but best understood as *Puritans*.

Both the Pharisees and the Zealots looked upon the acknowledgment of Caesar as king as sin. The Pharisees submitted to the Roman yoke as God's judgment, whilst the Zealots felt they were called upon to remove it by force. They refused to pay Roman taxes and were the cause of many uprisings. The destruction of Jerusalem in 70 AD was largely due to them. The Pharisees were a more "spiritual" movement. They were "Puritans" in many ways. They held family life to the authority of God's Word and the oral tradition (Talmud,) believed in minute and strict obedience to the Law as interpreted by the rabbis. They also

---

2 Luke 6:15 ASV
3 Philippians 3:5

believed in predestination, angels, future reward and judgment, and the resurrection of the body, etc.

They were very strict about defilement and food laws; a Pharisee could have a non-Pharisee to a meal but not vice versa! When a "sinner" came, he provided him with "clean" clothes! Anyone could become a Pharisee, and even though it was popular with the people, few joined because of the high standard required. The Pharisees gained control of the synagogues more or less. Modern Judaism traces its source to the Pharisees. We can get a wholly false idea of them! There is no doubt that we owe much to them, and that in its beginning it was a true movement of God. Furthermore we have to say that we can see the same characteristics again and again reappearing in church history in various appearances, including formalism, legalism, traditionalism, the outward more than the inward, the ritual more than the spiritual. Nicodemus[4], Joseph of Arimathea[5], Gamaliel[6], Saul of Tarsus[7] were all Pharisees.

Simon the Just

Then the Holy Spirit launched a spiritual movement through Simon the Just, one of the great figures of Jewish history. He singlehandedly saved Judaism from being totally submerged in Hellenism. That movement caused a return by the masses of the people to the Word of God, the purpose of God, and the Law of God. The Hebrew word from which we derive Pharisee means "to be separate." It was a kind of Separatist and Puritan movement.

4 John 3:1
5 Mark 15:43
6 Acts 5:34
7 Acts 23:6, 26:5; Philippians 3:5

It was a wholehearted return to the Lord Himself and it saved Israel from Hellenism and spiritual extinction. By the time of the New Testament, it had become, as so often is the case with genuinely spiritual movements, a legalistic and outward form of religion known as the Pharisees.

The Sadducees

The Sadducees on the other hand were never the numerous and popular movement that the Pharisees were. We find them a number of times in the gospel record[8] where they were almost completely comprised of wealthy upper-class and aristocratic people, and membership was not open to just anyone. The high priestly families and many of the priestly families were Sadducees. Originally, they were the Hellenized aristocracy of the land, and emerged at the same time as the Pharisees in the Maccabean period, the latter part of 2nd century BC.

On the whole they were rationalists, refusing to accept the oral law and the traditions, whereas the Pharisees put the oral law, which was the interpretation of the law by the elders and scribes, above the Law! They did not believe in a future life after judgment or in the resurrection[9] and angels[10]. The Law of Moses was the only accepted authority; even the prophets, they said, were simply "commentary." The Sadducees believed in free will which meant that men determined good and evil, and so forth. In later rabbinical writings the Sadducees were always looked upon as heretical. As a party they influenced the Roman

---

8 Matthew 22:23
9 Acts 4:1–2
10 Acts 5:17–19ff; 23:6–10

government greatly, and controlled the temple and the Sanhedrin. From the beginning there was a natural antipathy between them and the Pharisees, not to be wondered at. It is remarkable that they both united to destroy the Messiah[11]. Caiaphas, and Annas[12] were both high priests in the Sadducees that are mentioned in the New Testament.

The Essenes

The party of the Essenes grew up at the same time as the Pharisees and Sadducees, emerging from the Chasidim in the 2nd century BC. More than likely, they arose because they could not accept the political settlement after Antiochus IV Epiphanes, which gave the high priesthood and governorship to the Hasmoneans. They withdrew, therefore, from public life as a "righteous remnant," a "people prepared for the Lord."

Whereas both Pharisees and Sadducees were within public life, the Essenes believed in a complete separation and withdrawal. They entirely disagreed with the Sadducees, believing that the temple and its worship was polluted and compromised by them! They did not feel that the Pharisees were right in mixing with the multitude in worship. The Essenes appeared as a strange paradox. In many ways they were more legal and exacting than the Pharisees; yet at the same time they reacted against their formalism by moving to the more mystic inward view of all. They could be described as exclusive pietists.

As we have said, they went much farther than the Pharisees believing in complete separation. They built exclusive, highly

---

11 John 18:3, Matthew 27:62
12 John 18:3

organized communities and membership conditions were severe. It included renouncing money, taking no oaths, holding all property in common, pacifistic views. They were often celibate, although not always required. They were against slavery. They wore white garments as a symbol of purity and did not believe in animal sacrifice. They practiced a kind of regular baptism and had a 'fellowship meal' together. They had a fervent anticipation of the coming Messiah, believing that nothing but divine intervention in human affairs could allow God's purpose to be fulfilled. The community at Qumran expected three great figures to appear—namely, a prophet like Moses, a Davidic King and Messiah, and a great Aaronic priest. All three were fulfilled in the one person of Christ!

The Essenes stressed prophetic ministry in the Old Testament at the expense of the Law, believing that they had been given special insight into it. At times, we are told that there was prophesy among them and much ecstatic experience. Certainly they made a very great impression upon the common people. How they got the name *Essene*, we do not know. It possibly means "healers." Was the Qumran community where the Dead Sea scrolls were found Essene? Most scholars think so, although at present we cannot be dogmatic. There are striking similarities. From the evidence it would seem that there were many sects and groups such as these before Christ's coming which were covered by the name *Essene*. Although they are not mentioned in the New Testament, they played a great part in the preparation for the coming of the Messiah. It has been suggested that John the Baptist was greatly influenced by the Essenes; but we cannot be certain. The similarity between much of Christ's teaching, especially the

Sermon on the Mount, and Essene teaching has been pointed out too. It has even been suggested that the Passover Jesus observed was an Essene Passover which was held a few days earlier than the normally observed Passover.

The Scribes

The Scribes are a group we find mentioned many times in the New Testament. In fact they were another party among the Hebrews, located mainly in Judea, but were also found throughout the Dispersion. They were a body of men whose origins at least date back to Ezra. They were the experts in all matters to do with the Law of Moses. We find them called Scribes, "men of letters"— doctors, or teachers of the Law, and lawyers. Before Ezra's time it was an office combined with priesthood or Levitical service, but after the exile it was generally classed separate, although not always the case.

Ezra was the priest[13] and also the scribe[14]. There is no doubt that he left an indelible and abiding impression on this group. They were the creators of the synagogue service; they preserved the written form of the Oral Law, which eventually became the Talmud; and they preserved the Hebrew text of the Old Testament Scriptures in an utterly faithful way. In earlier days, before the New Testament, they were especially devoted to the study and exposition of the Law. They were editors, copyists, interpreters and students of the Word of God. They occupied themselves in collecting and editing the sacred writings of God's

13 Nehemiah 8:9
14 Ezra 7:6, 10

people. This included interpreting them in colloquial language to the common people who were largely ignorant of Hebrew after the return from Exile. We owe to the scribes, humanly speaking, I and II Chronicles, Ezra, Nehemiah and Esther. We can probably include Ecclesiastes and Proverbs to this list.

In the terrible persecutions under Antiochus Epiphanes they became a distinct political party and were granted seats in the Sanhedrin as a separate party alongside the chief priests and the elders. After this period they became more legalistic. Thus by New Testament times we find them as champions, perhaps unconsciously, of a formal legal piety. We find them in the New Testament associated more often than not with the Pharisees[15]. Basically they shared the same theological outlook, although the scribes were a separate class; and it would mean that there were scribes of the Sadducees as well.

In New Testament times they were divided into two schools— the School of Hillel, known for its mild and gentle interpretation of the Law; and the School of Shammai for its strictness, including the fact that they must not visit the sick, help the poor, or teach children on the Sabbath.

Hillel could have been one of the doctors with whom Christ discussed the Law at twelve years of age. There is a tradition that Shimeon who picked up Jesus in the temple[16] was in fact the son of Hillel and the Father of Gamaliel, who succeeded him as leader of his school.

The scribes' function was, therefore, threefold. Firstly, they were to preserve, explain and defend the Law of Moses.

15 Matthew 22:34–35
16 Luke 2:25–32

They did this by using the oral law to determine what the elders had said that the Law meant and required[17]. So important was this function that they were looked upon as "developing" the Law. Secondly, they taught pupils the Law throughout the land and the Dispersion. They lectured and debated in the temple[18]; hence the possibility that it was with them that Jesus discussed the Law at his Bar Mitzvah. Lastly, the scribes acted as judges in the administration of the Law in the Sanhedrin. They were usually addressed as "Rabbi," or "Father," or "Master." The term "rabbi" did not become a title until the 2nd century AD. The scribes in the New Testament are revealed to us as pedantic, fond of technicalities and discussion, lovers of honour, and holders of an outward and showy piety[19]. Matt 7:28–29 is also an interesting comment on them.

The greatest contribution the scribes made to Christ's coming was the editing, copying and collecting of Old Testament Scriptures, including the Hebrew text which is called the Masoretic, and is the basis of the present Old Testament. The form of the synagogue service, which they greatly influenced, may have contributed much to the early church's "pattern" of meeting.

---

17 Mark 7:1–13
18 Luke 2:46
19 Mark 12:38–40

3.
The Intertestamental Period–Part 3

The Synagogue

During the exile, God's people were forever cured of idolatry. With the temple destroyed, sacrifice ended, the Priesthood scattered, Jerusalem razed, the people deported, a new form of worship and fellowship grew up.

We do not know exactly how or when the synagogue started but somehow during the exile, God's children began gathering together for the reading and exposition of Scripture, and for worship and prayer. *Synagogue* is a Greek word meaning "a gathering of people," a congregation" (Hebrew Knesset). It is used fifty-six times in the New Testament.

Tradition ascribes its beginning to Ezekiel[1] and its development to Ezra. What we do know is that during the 400 years before Christ the synagogue became the greatest single factor in the life

---

1 Ezekiel 8:1; 20:1–3 cf 11:16

of the Jews, and even to this day the synagogue is the focal point of Jewish life.

Before the exile any such gathering was suspect because of the popular worship of "local" gods and the possibilities of this helping it. However, after the exile the synagogue became the recognized place for local Bible study and prayer, and the temple the place for sacrifice and great feasts.

Before a synagogue could be formed, there had to be ten males—thus Lydia's predicament. The synagogue was governed in a larger town by a body of twenty-three elders (Greek presbyters) and in smaller places, seven elders. This body was called a "Sanhedrin." They were sometimes called "rulers" or "shepherds." One called "the chief ruler" was first among equals.

Another important office was "the attendant" or "minister[2]." His job was to prepare the building as rooms for service, take the Scriptures needed to the person reading, teach the children and also inflict corporal punishment.

These elders or Sanhedrin served as the local court in Judea, both civil and religious. They could inflict three forms of punishment—namely, forty stripes save one, carried out in the synagogue by the attendant, excommunication[3] and death by stoning which required the Roman governor's assent. The Sanhedrin of Jerusalem became known as the Great Sanhedrin—the highest court and authority among Jews, recognized throughout the land and the dispersion.

The synagogue building was simple. The chief piece of furniture was the ark in which the rolls of Scripture were kept.

---

2 Luke 4:20
3 Greek "anathema" – absolute and final exclusion; or temporary loss of privilege etc.

It was normally placed in front of the wall farthest from the entrance. In the larger buildings there was a platform in the centre with a lectern upon it. The rest of the room was used for seating, the chief seats being near the ark.

In the synagogue worship any competent Jew of age could contribute under the supervision of the chief ruler. The service consisted of prayer, reading of Law and of prophets, and the translation and exposition of Scripture. Normally it was a scribe who would be called upon to preach or teach. All contributions were made from the platform. To read you stood, to teach you sat, and for prayer all stood normally with arms outstretched. The synagogue acted as a library and a school.

The synagogues main contributions for Christ's coming were the intense regular reading and teaching of Scripture which kept alive the Word of God, the sense of His purpose, and of Messiah's coming. Equally tremendous was the impact upon the Gentile world throughout the Dispersion. They were strategic centres already prepared for the gospel. The synagogue's simple pattern and way of meeting influenced the early Christians under God.

The Great Sanhedrin

We have already mentioned the Sanhedrin, but further mention should be made. The Great Sanhedrin was the highest and most authoritative court and assembly in Jewry before and during the time of Christ. Comprising some seventy councillors, it is referred to in the New Testament as "the Council,"[4] "the body or assembly of elders"[5] or "the Senate."[6]

According to the traditions it began with the seventy elders in Moses' day[7] and was reorganized and reinstated by Ezra after the return from exile. However, we do not really know how it began. The Persians certainly constituted some such body under the governor who administered "home rule" for Judea.

In the Greek period a senate was permitted which represented the whole nation and was made up of aristocratic elders. During the Roman period this became known as the Sanhedrin, and the whole internal government of the land was in its hands under the watchful eye of the Roman Procurator. Whilst beyond the land, throughout the Dispersion, its authority was recognized.

Originally the Sanhedrin was comprised of the Sadducean priestly aristocracy. From Ezra's day civil and religious authority were in the hands of the high priest. Thus the priestly nobility were the leading people of the nation. During the 1st century BC the Pharisees and the scribes were both admitted and given seats. In earlier days it was mainly Sadducean, but under Herod the Pharisees grew in strength and the Sadducees were restricted.

By New Testament times the Sanhedrin was made up of three groups.[8] These three groups included the chief priests, also known as the high priests, acting and previous, and members of priestly nobility, along with the elders including both tribal and family heads, and finally the legal experts of the day known as scribes.

---

4 Matthew 26:59
5 Luke 22:66; Acts 22:5
6 Acts 5:21
7 Numbers 11:16,17
8 Mark 15:1

All three groups belonged to either the Pharisees (mainly elders & scribes) or the Sadducees (mainly chief priests and aristocracy)

The Sanhedrin had two main areas of responsibility which were the administrative and judicial[9], as well as the religious. It had either the sole right of judgment upon especially important matters or was appealed to by the local Sanhedrin when they were unable to come to a decision.

When in session they sat in a semi-circle in order to see one another in debate. There were no sessions on Sabbaths or Holy Days. Two clerks sat before them, one to count the "nos," the other "yeas." Twenty-three members was the quorum for a session. A majority of two was necessary for condemnation, but just one for acquittal.

The Temple

The temple of Christ's time was in fact neither Solomon's nor Zerubbabel's. And it would be well to trace the history of the temple during these four hundred years. Going right back to the tabernacle and representing the eternal purpose of God to dwell in the midst of His own was not only the focal point of the life of His people and of their progress, but also of conflict.

Solomon's Temple

Solomon's temple was a magnificent structure. It was a copy of the tabernacle with its dimensions doubled and provided for by David and built by Solomon. Nebuchadnezzar destroyed it after

---

9 Cases of capital punishment required the Roman Procurator's consent

about four hundred years in 587 BC, and the furniture and holy vessels were removed to Babylon and placed in a heathen temple.

Zerubbabel's temple

In 536 BC Cyrus not only allowed the people to return but he sent back the holy vessels for the new temple which was to be built. The ark however had disappeared forever. This new temple was not built on the grand scale of Solomon's. Nevertheless, it was no small feat. It was in this temple that Haggai and Zechariah ministered to the people.[10]

In 168 BC Antiochus Epiphanes robbed and desecrated this temple. He took away the brazen vessels and erected an altar and statue to Jupiter on the brazen altar. Three years later Judas Maccabaeus led the Jews to victory, retaking Jerusalem in which there was a cleansing and rededicating of the temple.

In 63 BC Pompey conquered Jerusalem for Rome, but did not rob the temple, though he entered the Holiest Place. Nine years later Crassus took away many of the more valuable things. In 37 BC Herod (later the great!) stormed the temple and burnt some of its walls.

Herod's Temple

Herod the Great, who was an Edomite, in the 18th year of his reign, about 19 BC, due to conscience and a desire to reconcile the Jews to himself, and to raise a memorial to himself, began the rebuilding of the temple. This building work stretched

10 Haggai 1, 2, 3; Zechariah 4:6–10, and also Malachi; see Malachi 3:1

over years. John 2:20 tells us that it had taken some forty-six years and was not finished. In fact the actual sanctuary took nine years but all the additions were not completed until 64 AD, only six years before it was forever destroyed in 70 AD.

This temple was exceedingly impressive. The eastern front of the sanctuary itself was covered with plates of gold, which caught the rays of the rising sun, and could be seen for miles. The stone that was used was white marble, and a large part of the sidewalls were also covered with gold. The whole temple area covered twice the space of Zerubbabel's, and this area had to be filled up in order to be used. A battlemented wall of massive stone blocks, averaging four feet high and fifteen feet long, surrounded the whole site.

A large outer court called the *court of the Gentiles* into which Gentiles were allowed surrounded the inner court and sanctuary. This court was surrounded on the inside of the massive walls by two rows of pillars on three sides and three rows on the fourth. These had a wooden roof, and they were made into porticoes or cloisters in which the scribes held their schools and debates, and the merchants and moneylenders had their stalls.

Solomon's porch was on the east wall, and the royal porch was on the south. From the court of the Gentiles one passed into the inner court with the warnings clearly shown to non-Jews in Greek and Latin. This inner court was raised somewhat above the outer. One passed immediately into the women's court, in which were the chests for gifts, and beyond which no woman was allowed. From the women's court one entered into the court of the Israelites and then into the priest's court, in which was the brazen altar. These courts were all raised above the others, till you came to the sanctuary itself. The gates of these courts were for the most part overlaid with silver and gold.

In the priest's court, if you were to look up and see the great door to the sanctuary, you would see a pure gold vine at its top. Thus the rising sun would catch the golden front of the temple and its golden vine every day.

On the northwest corner of the outer court was the fortress of Antonia, where the Roman garrison was stationed and where the Roman Procurator stayed when in Jerusalem.

This was the temple Christ came to and fulfilled.

4.
The Intertestamental Period–Part 4

The Canon of the Old Testament and Other Jewish Literature

During the four hundred years before Christ, we discover three main streams of literary activity. Firstly, was the *Canon of the Old Testament*. We use the term canon meaning "measure" to distinguish from other writings that are divinely inspired and absolutely authoritative.

The canon, by the time of Christ, the TaNaKh (Old Testament Scriptures) was fully recognized in the three fold Jewish arrangement consisting of *Torah* (Law), *Neviim* (Prophets), and *Ketuvim* (Writings).[1] No council at any time "canonized" these Scriptures. They only recognized what was universally accepted as divinely inspired. From the beginning the Law of Moses was fully accepted. By Ezra's day the prophets had been for the most

---

1 Luke 24:44 cf. Luke 11:51

part accepted. By the 2nd century BC they were fully recognized, except for Ezekiel over which there was discussion.

It was *The Writings*, which give the most difficulty. It seems reasonably certain that they had been given full recognition by Christ's day. As late as 70 AD there was heated discussion upon Esther, Ecclesiastes, Song of Songs, and Proverbs, but this would infer widespread acceptance. The result of these discussions was the absolute acceptance of these books as canonical. Thus during these years the Old Testament took the essential form known to us.

The Apocryphal Literature

Secondly, they had *the Apocryphal Literature*. Strictly speaking the Apocrypha is a varied assortment of Jewish literature from 300 BC to 100 AD not included in the Hebrew Old Testament nor recognized by the scribes or later rabbis. In the Septuagint, (the Greek translation of the Old Testament often referenced by the Roman numeral LXX—(see "The Languages Used" below) however, these were included and this was one more source of friction between the Hellenists and the Hebrews. Yet we have to say that whilst the canonical books have been universally accepted, the Apocrypha has not. Hellenists wrote much of it under the assumed names of Old Testament characters.

The Tradition of the Elders

The *Tradition of the Elders*[2] was the teaching handed down from master to disciple. Between the Testaments there was much explanation and elaboration upon the Old Testament, especially the Law. Jewish tradition says it was the elders of Moses' day that started it and the scribes developed it. By New Testament times the *Tradition of the Elders* had been placed alongside the Scriptures and made as authoritative as them. In this way the Word of God was often contradicted and "set at nought." Finally the *Tradition of the Elders* became the basis of *The Talmud*.

The Languages Used

The Bible is written in three languages, Hebrew, Aramaic and Greek. Most of the Old Testament is in Hebrew, some small passages are in Aramaic, and the whole New Testament is in Greek.

During the 400 years before Christ, Aramaic became the language of God's people instead of Hebrew, and Greek became the universal language of the civilized world.

Aramaic is not derived from Hebrew, but belongs to the same family, being very close to it and using the same script. It seems that it was the diplomatic language of the Assyrian Empire and continued through the Persian Empire till its end in 331 BC.

After the exile it gradually superseded Hebrew as the spoken language of the Promised Land until, in New Testament times, it was universally spoken by the Hebrews. Thus Christ's mother

---

2 See Mark 7:3, 5

tongue, as was all the apostles, was Aramaic. Hebrew remained the "sacred language" (rather like R.C. Latin) used by the scribes in discussion and for writing.

Greek was the other great language of the Bible. From 331 BC Greek gradually became the common language of the empire, until in New Testament times it was *the* universal tongue. This Greek was not classical Greek nor modern Greek, but it is often called "Hellenistic Greek." In most of the Dispersion, the Hellenists spoke Greek and it was into this Greek that they translated the Old Testament in what we now call the Septuagint (LXX). Later all the writings that were to form the New Testament were written in this Greek.

God's Land

We need to say something about the history of the Promised Land during these 400 years, and how the administrative districts and local character and differences evolved. When the Jews returned to Judah in 586 BC, they controlled a very small area, more or less the tribal area of Judah, within the Persian Empire. Over this area they were given home rule. There was a gradual expansion southwards and eastwards, with Jewish communities coming into being throughout the land. This gradual expansion continued through the Greek era.

During the Maccabean period, 2nd century BC, there was a taking over almost completely of the original territory of Israel.

In 64 BC Pompey conquered Syria, making it an Imperial Province directly responsible to The Emperor.

In 63 BC Judea was incorporated into the Roman Provinces of Syria. Thus all Jewish resettlements were included. It was a border province on the eastern boundary of the Roman Empire, on the south and southeast was the Nabatean Kingdom with its capital at Petra; and on the east, the Parthians. Because of the Parthian threat particularly, Rome kept Syria as an Imperial Province, instead of a senatorial one.

In the days of Herod the Great 37–4 BC, the Jews were given home rule within the Imperial Province of Syria under the watchful eye of the legate (or governor) of Syria. The territory had expanded north-eastwards, but shrunk in the south. At Herod's death much dissension in what remained of his family, was settled when the Emperor split up the territory amongst his sons. He gave Samaria, Judea and N. Idumea to Archelaus; Galilee and Perea to Herod Antipas; the region east of Upper Jordan to Philip, afterwards called the Tetrarchy of Philip.

When serious charges were made against Archelaus to Augustus by a delegation of Judeans and Samaritans, he deposed him in 6 AD and made Samaria, Judea, and N. Idumea a kind of sub-imperial Province under a Roman Procurator with the administrative seat at Caesarea.

Caesarea was a beautiful and attractive place, thoroughly Hellenized, with a man-made harbour and a fine royal palace. This palace was the Procurator's residence. He only went up to Jerusalem at feasts and when needed, and he stayed at Herod the Great's palace.

This province of Judea was always under the watchful eye of the governor (legate) of Syria. Thus Pontius Pilate was the fifth in line of the Judean Procurators under the senior Syrian Legate. In fact, in 36 AD the Syrian governor sent Pilate to Rome to stand trial on a charge of unfair dealings with The Samaritans.

When Judea became a province, Gaza and district were detached and made part of the Province of Syria. Thus the Holy Land was split up into a number of regions either directly under the Syrian governor, or the Judean. It would seem that the governor of Syria had overall military supervision and respectability. These districts were split into a number of regions.

Samaria, Judea and North Idumea

This, as we have said, constituted the Imperial Province of Judea with its capital at Caesarea.

Judea

There is not much need to say something about Judea. Judeans felt they were *the* people and looked upon themselves as city folk, cultured, refined, spiritually elite and living at the centre and heart of things in the area which witnessed so much of God's working, and where historically there has been the least decline and the most revivals! Here was the least Gentile and Greek influence found and the most Jewish!

Idumea[3]

These were the old Edomites, who had settled in South Judea as they were pushed out of Edom proper by the Nabataeans (descendants of Ishmael, modern Arabs). They had been subdued in the Maccabean period and compelled to be circumcised. Thus they were Judaised Edomites or Edomite Jews! Herod the Great was the son of an Idumean Father and Nabatean Mother. He married a Jewess. One can therefore understand the Pharisees feelings about the "mixed multitude."

Samaria

Samaria first appears in the Old Testament as the name of the capital of the northern kingdom of Israel during the division. When Israel fell in 721 BC and Samaria was taken, most of the upper classes were deported to other areas of the Assyrian Empire, and non-Jewish people were deported to and settled in Israel. Thus a mixed population grew up with a kind of worship recognizing Jehovah as supreme but recognizing other Gods and rites.[4]

When the remnant returned to rebuild the temple etc., these Samaritans caused much trouble. They had a temple on Mt. Gerazim, an "apostate" priesthood, and a sacrificial system, etc. They possessed the Law but not the prophets.

At the time of Antiochus Epiphanes, when the Jews resisted to death his attempts to corrupt the temple, the Samaritans compromised fully and dedicated their temple to Zeus. Herod the Great's favourite seat was Samaria, which he rebuilt as a

---

3 see Mark 3:8
4 see II Kings 17:24–33

Hellenistic city with a beautiful temple on the hill above it, dedicated to Augustus. All this did not make for harmony between Jews and Samaritans. The real point of the controversy was, however, the temple at Mt. Gerizim.

By New Testament times the Samaritans had six basic articles of beliefs. They believed in one God, Moses the prophet, the Law, Mt. Gerizim as the place appointed by God for worship and sacrifice, the Day of Judgment and the coming Prophet or Restorer.

The bitterness between Jew and Samaritan grew in intensity through many incidents till in the days of Christ there were *no* intercessors at all, and Jews were not even travelling through Samaria if they could help it.[5] It is therefore interesting to note the Lord's attitude to them e.g. the good Samaritan; the Samaritan woman, the Samaritan who returned to give thanks, etc. It is also noteworthy how real a response to the gospel there was among the Samaritans.

The Tetrarchy of Philip

This region northeast of the Lake of Galilee, was made up of at least five districts, and was ruled by Philip, the most just and conscientious of Herod's sons, under the Syrian Legate. It was essentially the area known as "Bashan" in the Old Testament.

The whole area was prevailingly Gentile. Philip built Caesarea Philippi, a completely Hellenistic city. He also rebuilt Bethsaida on Lake Galilee as his capital. Philip the apostle came from Bethsaida.[6]

---

5 see John 4:9
6 see Mark 6:45; 8:22, 27; John 12:21

The Decapolis

Decapolis means literally "ten cities" and was the name given to a federation of Hellenistic cities. This league of Gentile type cities came under Roman protection after Pompey took Syria. The Decapolis was incorporated into the Province of Syria.

It was a loose federation numbering probably more than ten, and some of its cities were outside of the Decapolis e.g. Damascus. They probably bonded together to defend their culture and traditions against Jewish and Semitic influences. It covered the old tribal area of Manasseh, and was the most Gentile of all the areas of the Promised Land.[7]

Galilee and Peraea

Herod Antipas governed the two districts of Galilee and Peraea. He appears to us in the Gospels as the Tetrarch Herod. They were not in the Province of Judea, but in the Province of Syria, although granted home rule. Rulers in part of a Roman Province were called "Tetrarchs."[8]Herod executed John the Baptist and Christ called him "that fox" in Luke 13:32.

Peraea corresponded approximately to the old Gilead. Although attractive, it was more thinly populated. Through its territory ran the "all Jewish" road from Galilee to Judea. It is always referred to in the New Testament as "beyond the Jordan."[9]

Galilee means, "ring" "circle" "circuit," hence "region." It comprised the old tribal area of Naphtali, Zebulun, Asher,

---

7 see Mark 5:20; 7:35; Matthew 4:25
8 see Matthew 14:1; Luke 3:19, 23:6–7 ff
9 see Matthew 4:25; John 1:28; 10:40

and Issachar. It is divided into upper and lower Galilee (rabbis spoke of Tiberias as the third division).

Upper Galilee is mostly over 3000 ft. and in one place rising to 9230 ft. Here is the magnificent scenery, wild and remote. Lower Galilee, below 2000 ft., drops off to Lake Galilee situated below sea level. It is beautiful fertile country, a district of wooded hills, olive orchards and vineyards. In spring the hills were ablaze with flowers and the valleys covered with grain.[10] Galilee is therefore essentially an upland area. Its fertility was renowned—"if anyone wishes to be rich, let him go north; if wise, let him go south."

Gilboa, little Hermon, Tabor, Carmel, the plain of Jezreel were all in Galilee whilst snow covered the Hermon. Rising to 9300 ft. it dominated everything from a distance. Here were Capernaum, Tiberias, Chorazin, Gennesaret, Magdala, Nazareth, Cana, and Naim.

Herod Antipas built Tiberias as his capital. It was very Hellenistic and shunned by local Jews. Thus the Lake of Galilee is sometimes called "Sea of Tiberias."

Nazareth lies in a high valley among the southerly hills of the Lebanon range. The valley floor is 1200m and steep hills rise up on north and east, and on the west reach 1600m. Main roads passed nearby Nazareth.

It would seem that temperamentally Galileans were more "Latin" than the Judeans. They were supposed to be more rebellious, high-spirited, quarrelsome, and hot-blooded. Josephus tells us they were hard working, manly people. They were certainly practical in outlook and known to be less Pharisee.

10 see Geography of Bible, Baly p. 190

They spoke with a definite provincial accent being unable to pronounce the gutturals.[11] They also dressed in a provincial way. To the more urbane and refined Judean, this was "countrified," "lower class," "rural!" Added to all that was the isolation of the Galilee, cut off from Judea by Samaria, surrounded by Gentiles and Hellenised. It was called "Galilee of the Gentiles,"[12] Gentile incursions and influences made it suspect and despised in Judean eyes.

The rabbis said, "Judea is grain, Galilee straw, beyond chaff." Thus it was despised.[13] Yet it was here that the Messiah was to live and work. The main part of His life was spent in Nazareth (30 years) as a carpenter; the main centre of His ministry was Capernaum; the main part of His ministry was exercised north and west of Lake Galilee.

Most of the older disciples were Galileans—Peter, Andrew, James, John; and Matthew, who was the Customs Officer, or Tax Gatherer at Capernaum;[14] Nathaniel came from Cana[15] where Christ performed his first miracle;[16] also where the Centurion came about his son.[17] Mary Magdalene was from Magdala (city of dyes), famed for its wool industry, shops and corruption.[18]

For consider your calling, brethren, that there were not many wise according to the flesh, not many mighty, not many noble; but God has chosen the foolish things of the world to shame the

---

11 see Mark 14:70; Matthew 26:73; Acts 2:7
12 see Isaiah 9:1
13 see John 1:46, John 7:41, 52
14 see Matthew 9:9
15 see John 21:2
16 see John 2:1–11
17 see Matthew 8:5–13
18 see Mark 15:40

wise, and God has chosen the weak things of the world to shame the things which are strong, and the base things of the world and the despised God has chosen, the things that are not, so that He may nullify the things that are, so that no man may boast before God. [19]

---

19 I Corinthians 1:26–29 (NASB)

5.
The Intertestamental Period–Part 4a

The Little Horn–The Antichrist

The whole period from the Persian King Cambyses 530 BC to the Maccabees in 165 BC was predicted and foretold by Daniel. So detailed were his predictions that some could only believe that they were history written up under the guise of prophecy.[1]

Even more remarkable is that the predictions finish before the glorious era of the Maccabees, as if inferring that we are meant to understand something more than the period of history from 530 BC to 165 BC.

The period is thus set forth as prophetic of "the end," and Antiochus Epiphanes becomes the symbol and archetype in Scripture of the antichrist. Thus, as before Christ's First Advent there was great apostasy, cultural floundering, antichrist and tribulation, so before His Second Advent there will be also!

---

1 see Scroggie, Unfolding Drama of Redemption Vol. II Pp17–25

This is seen by a comparison of the visions in Daniel concerning the "Little Horn." It immediately becomes apparent that the "Little Horn" is someone to come at the end of the 4th empire; and yet it is Antiochus Epiphanes who is enlarged upon in the succeeding visions.

When we come to Revelation, there are some interesting comparisons. In Daniel 2 there are ten toes, part iron, and part clay, and Daniel 7 describes a beast having ten horns. The dragon of Revelation 12:3 has seven heads, seven crowns (diadems), ten horns and meets the beast in Revelation 13:1. Out of ten horns in Dan 7:24 the little horn emerges, and out of seven heads in Revelation 13:1 the 7th head becomes the 8th.[2]

What does *antichrist* mean then? It can mean "against Christ" or "instead of Christ." Probably both are right as he sets himself up in Christ's place, and thus opposes him. Antichrist should not be confused with *false Christs* in Matthew 24:24 which literally means "pseudo Christs."

We find "antichrist" called by a number of names in Scripture. These include the antichrist,[3] the man of sin, the son of perdition,[4] he that opposes God,[5] the lawless one,[6] the beast,[7] and finally, the little horn.[8]

Is antichrist a system, or a person, or an influence?[9] He is all three. Supremely he is the person who heads a system,

---

2 Revelation 13.3 cf. 17:10
3 I John 2:18
4 II Thessalonians 2:3
5 II Thessalonians 2:4
6 II Thessalonians 2:8
7 Revelation 11:7, cf 17:8, 11
8 Daniel 7:8
9 I John 2:18, cf 4:3; II John 7

a superhuman figure embodying man's genius and strength. He is a demonic leader of mankind, effectively the devil's Christ, entitled simply as Satan's desire of all nations.

Antichrist is also a system called "the beast." This is a great political, economic, religious system, and it is, as he is, the flowering and painting of the mystery of lawlessness[10] and the spirit of antichrist,[11] which have always been in the world. It is the resulting product of the dragon, the devil himself.

Who is antichrist himself? Is he a mere man with evil ideas? Or a man possessed by evil spirits? Or by the devil himself? Or is he an incarnation of the devil?[12] It is quite amazing to note the comparison between Christ and the antichrist in Scripture.

What can we learn from the Intertestament period, and particularly from Antiochus Epiphanes about the antichrist? Satan's object is to create such a mess in the covenant people, complicating things by every possible means that God will give up and in doing so he would prevent Christ's coming and his own final undoing.

Antichrist is Satan's last great energetic and brilliant thrust, his last great apparition to stop Christ. By that period, and what precedes it immediately, is an attempt to corrupt the church and use it as a satanic tool. Indeed, Satan purposes to create a false, counterfeit church to simulate signs and wonders confusing believers and deluding unbelievers, and finally to wipe out the true church intimidating those on the fringe or living in the shallows.

---

10 II Thessalonians 2:7
11 I John 4:3
12 II Thessalonians 2:3, cf Judas Iscariot John 17:12; II Thessalonians 2:9; Revelation 13:4; Daniel 8:24.

Thus the whole battle is centred upon the true church in its building up and its completion. The Bridegroom is beyond Satan's reach; it is therefore to the bride, His body, that Satan turns. That final great onslaught has been prepared for our centuries, just as in the Intertestamental period. Satan will seek to corrupt worship, incorporate Babylonian practice, impose Hellenic culture and engage the arm of flesh, all to seek to rob the church from within. Satan seeks to destroy the heavenliness, the spirituality, the divine character of God's people in order to make it but a human society or club, humanly sustained, governed, and energized.

In short, Satan's plan is to "take over" the church. Looking at the church in the New Testament and what we are today we can see how successful his preparations have been!! For that "take-over attempt" he is preparing apostates and traitors ready to compromise in the day of tribulation (e.g. James, Menelaus).[13]

Antichrist, like Antiochus Epiphanes, may well be democratic, genial, affable and popular. In this way he will take in the whole world.[14]

We may well learn from the policy of Antiochus Epiphanes that antichrist will be similarly "enlightened," desiring unity politically, economically and religiously. All this will be carried out under a guise in order to reunify and ban war, pooling resources for the common good of man.

Surely we can see already the watchword everywhere: "UNITY." Anything which divides is wrong. Political unity is under discussion everywhere as is economic unity! Historic attempts

13 Daniel 11:30–31
14 Daniel 7:8, 20; 8:23; Revelation 13:4, 8, Revelation 17:13; II Thessalonians 2:11

have been made already. A few recent examples include Napoleon, Hitler, Mussolini, Stalin, Churchill, the "Common Market" and now the UN and EU.

Whether this system will include the whole world, every nation, is not absolutely clear. The beast will have worldwide influence and power even if the system does not include every country. We do know that religious unity is one of the objections. And have we not seen in the last few years something like a miracle taking place before our eyes–Anglicans joining Catholics; reunion schemes; 2nd Vatican Council, etc. The aim is a world church. In the time of Antiochus Epiphanes the temple became a corrupt "counterfeit" with an apostate high priest, apostate priesthood, so that its very worship and service became the expression of that apostasy.

"Apostasy" means "abandonment of true faith, vows, principles, etc." That apostasy in 175 BC was but the foreshadowing of the harlot and the false prophet of Revelation, and Satan's final great attempt to "take over" the church of God.

The Counterfeit Church

The creation of that "counterfeit church" is the result of the great apostasy foretold in II Thessalonians 2:3 and II Tim 4:1 involving "seducing spirits" and "doctrines of demons" described in Revelation 16:13–14.

This great harlot (once pure now defiled) and the false prophet will be the willing tools of the beast. Note that the beast carries the harlot; she is "supported and carried along." Without him she has no real power! It seems reasonably clear that this harlot is a religious system centred in the political capital of the beast.

Can she be identified? She causes martyrs and saint's blood to be spilled in her.[15] She creates state unions[16] and even Roman Catholics have always identified Revelation 17:9 with Rome. It seems to me we have nominal Christendom reunited in Rome, wedded to the state and wielding political power.

The false prophet "represents" the Lamb, but speaks for Satan![17] It would seem he symbolizes the leadership of this counterfeit church. Certainly he uses all his supernatural powers to support and carry out the policies of the antichrist.[18]

He makes it impossible for anyone to conduct a living unless they are registered. The system has a kind of vast Trade Union with a "closed shop" policy.[19] Indeed, he is the means of many being deceived and deluded, and true believers being eliminated. Thus will antichrist take his place in the temple of God.[20]

This is why the Word of God is so absolutely dogmatic upon this matter! Christians are to break their connection with the harlot.[21] Now it will be the true church unadulterated that will present antichrist with his great problem! The true church will be unreasonable, stubborn, short-sighted, narrow-minded, old-fashioned, bigots and divisionists, frustrating his policy everywhere. If they increase it means more trouble! Therefore they must be stopped.

---

15 Revelation 17:6, cf 18:24
16 Revelation 17:2, 18
17 Revelation 13:4, cf. Revelation 16:13
18 Revelation 13:12–15
19 Rev 13:16–17
20 II Thessalonians 2:4
21 Revelation 18:4, cf II Corinthians 6:14–7:1

The fact that so many "Christians" included in the historic denominations are supporting him puts such believers in an even worse light. These people are unreasonable, so divisive, that they will not even join with other Christians in the one Christian World Church! This reveals how perverted their teaching must be!

They hold and teach belief not in keeping with the spirit of the times. They will not even consider that they may be wrong. Thus for antichrist and the false prophet *The Final Solution* is that these believers must either be made to see reason or wiped out. This will occasion the most terrible persecution in world history, otherwise known as the great tribulation, of which all that has preceded prior to this has been a mere shadow.[22]

It is the last final attempt of Satan to frustrate Christ's coming by simply annihilating the church. He will throw every reserve, every ounce of energy into this last onslaught. Furthermore, God will let him go to lengths to which he has never before been permitted.[23] It is during this time that the "Abomination of Desolation" appears in the temple itself.[24]

In connection with this period of terrible tribulation the figure three and one half appears again and again. It is true that the period of persecution under Antiochus Epiphanes lasted about seven years, and that the terrible and fiercest phase lasted three

---

22 Daniel 12:1; Matthew 24:2
23 Daniel 8:24–25 ARSV
24 Daniel 11:31; Matt 24:15 cf Mark 13:14, note "he" RV. ASV cf, also II Thessalonians
   2:3–4

and one half years. Are we to take this figure symbolically or literally?[25] We must rejoice that these days will be shortened.[26]

We have learned all this about the antichrist from Antiochus Epiphanes. Does his origin or sphere give us any indication as to where he will arise? Greece? Egypt? Certainly there is one or more things we ought to note and that is the speed and suddenness of both his appearance and success.[27] If it is true that we are living in the last time, the antichrist must soon appear! Have we any indication at all?[28]

The True Church Is Completed

Above and beyond everything else, the Intertestament period proclaims the absolute sovereignty of God, even at the worst and most satanically inspired moments. It declares the glorious triumph of God over Satan and his antichrist![29]

Satan and his antichrist, with all their seeming success, do not have a chance. There is an "until," a "but," a "time appointed," and a "yet."[30] During this very time when Satan seems to have succeeded, a purified remnant will be brought out and in them and through them the Lord will complete His purpose.[31] We must also rejoice that the martyr number is fixed; it will "be completed!"[32]

---

25 Revelation 13:5; 11:2–3 (9); 12:6, 14; Daniel 7:25, 12:7, 11–12
26 Matthew 24:22
27 Daniel 11:21–24 ARS
28 Read from "Gift of prophecy" by Ruth Montgomery. Pages 175, 177, 178, 180, 181, 193. The source of this gift is evil but probably correct.
29 Daniel 7:9–14 cf 2:34, 44.
30 Daniel 7:22, 26–27 8:25, 11:27, 35, 45
31 Daniel 11:32, 33, 35, 12:1, 10; Revelation 7:13–17, 12:11, 15:2–4
32 Revelation 6:9–11

The glory of the latter house will succeed the former! The church at the end will correspond to the church at the beginning if only in a remnant! The bride will have made herself ready!

The devil will have no satisfaction at all! What God has set out to have from the beginning—a people in eternal union with His Son—He has achieved. There will be no defeat as far as God is concerned.

We have not said anything about the rapture of the saints over which there is so much discussion. But this we can say, and say dogmatically, that when the true church is completed, Christ, the top stone, will appear, and His own—His faithful, purified, suffering people—will be gloriously taken!

And if Isaiah 28:16 predicted the coming of Christ, His work and objective, then Zechariah 4:7 (cf. 3:9) speaks of His coming again.[33] Suddenly in a moment of time we shall be taken.[34] Will all be taken? Let us watch and pray!

The encouragement we gain from this Intertestament period is that neither Antiochus Epiphanes nor his reign of terror, nor his policies, nor an apostate temple, traitorous spiritual leaders, nor corrupted worship, nor a compromised covenant people, and not even Satan himself could or did stop Christ coming!

Christ the Overcomer

He came in due time, not early and certainly not late! There came a certain point in time when a star appeared, unique

---

33 Titus 2:13–14
34 1 Thessalonians 4:15–17; I Corinthians 15:51–52; Matthew 24:40–42

for its brightness and position. It was the herald of the Messiah in an unsuspecting world.

There in some smelly, dingy, little, cow-stable, among the very beasts themselves, in a squalid, and for the most part unknown, little Middle-Eastern town, unsought for and unrecognized except by a faithful handful, God appeared in the flesh. It was *the miracle*, eclipsing all the miracles that had preceded it, the point to which all history had moved, and the day which Satan had done all to avert. Christ had come!

Whatever we may feel about December 25th—and there are many conflicting theories—the day we celebrate the official, though not actual, birthday of Christ, was originally chosen because it was "the birthday of the unconquered Sun;" the day it began to be apparent that light was conquering darkness by the lengthening of day.[35]

And if Christ came then in due time, so will it be at the end of this age! Neither antichrist, nor his policies, nor tribulation, nor the beast, nor the false prophet with his lying wonders, nor the deluded nations, nor an apostate church, nor apostate Christian leaders will stop, or can stop Christ's coming again. He will come, and will come on time. Does not Peter refer to this very thing in II Peter 1:19?

Perhaps the most amazing thing is that when Satan is doing his worst and the persecution is the most terrible, Christ is seen unperturbed upon the throne of God. This is a feature in the book of Revelation!

The fact is that *Christ is the Overcomer!!* He has won. Now He waits, enthroned! So tremendous is this fact that God allows,

35 John 1:4, 5

almost encourages Satan to do his work. The devil is beaten. God finally uses even his activity to fulfil His own purpose! Thus in Satan's ear the bell has tolled steadily through the centuries of church history, and is tolling today, signalling his defeat and end!

It began with the cry of Christ upon the cross: "FINISHED!" It tore the veil in the Temple in two, and rang throughout Hell, like a sword piercing the heart of Satan. It has never stopped tolling until it will break into triumphant peals ringing out the coming of God's kingdom, and final victory over all evil.

Maybe its tones at times have been muffled, but it rings on. During the last phase of world history, when it will seem that Satan is visibly evident and visually victorious, that bell will ring through the true church never more clearly!

It heralds not Satan's, nor antichrist's but *God's final solution.* [36]

---

36 Revelation 19:1–8 NEB

6.
The Intertestamental Period–Part 5

The History of the Intertestamental Period

We come now to a brief survey of the history of this period, dwelling particularly upon the time of Antiochus Epiphanes and the Macabees.

Zerubbabel was the last of the royal princes of the house of David to take any office. The actual throne of David became vacant when King Zedekiah was taken into exile in 586 BC; there was no rightful, legal king or prince in Israel until Christ was born.

In this long period the high priests became the rulers, combining both civil and religious authority. This was an altogether new feature in the life of God's people.

Saladin has given us a glimpse of the corrupt and compromised condition of the priesthood at the beginning of this era. With few exceptions it entwined to deteriorate until Annas and Caiaphas (Luke 3:2) of the New Testament. So corrupt did it become that the high priesthood was more or less "sold" to the highest bidder on a number of occasions! It became a veritable tool for the enemy more than once.

Over this period, and especially after Alexander the Great's death, the Promised Land became the cockpit of the struggles between the two major factions in the empire—Egypt and Syria. The control of the land to a certain extent meant the control of the Dispersion Jews as well as the control of many of the old trade routes and highways.

Above and beyond all, it was the period when the enemy's essential and supreme objective was the hindering and frustrating of the Messiah's coming. Everything in his armory was thrown into a tremendous battle to nullify God's Purpose.

Thus this whole period was a battlefield, touching depths of utter darkness, wickedness, and satanic cruelty, and heights of pure faith, heroic martyrdom, suffering, and triumph. By every means Satan sought to make it impossible for God to act by seeking to compromise the priesthood and the high priest, making them tools of Satan instead of God. He Hellenised the people of God through Greek influence, thought, culture, language, dress etc., destroying the testimony, corrupting the true worship and service of God by Greek philosophy and religion. Another of his strategies was to press God's people into legalism (Pharisees) or subjectionism (Essenes), and create Gentile centres in the land itself, effectually making the whole thing—land, people, temple, priesthood—such a mess that God would give it all up! But God triumphed, and the stone not made with hands hurtled out of heaven to fulfil the redeeming purpose of God, and smash, in the end, the prince of this world and his kingdom into pulp.

Has not, therefore, this period a tremendous amount to teach us who await the Messiah's final appearing? Can we not see that this period is a battlefield, and will become so with ever growing intensity? Is it not clear to us that Satan is seeking to frustrate the coming of our Lord Jesus, attacking the true church—its unity, its distinctiveness, its functioning, its development, its building up, its completion? By every means available he works to undo the work and purpose of God. But God will win!

Let us then proceed to study this period more closely. The pre-Maccabean period extends from the end of the Old Testament Canon to the rise of Antiochus Epiphanes approximately 445 BC to 175 BC, a period of 270 years. This period was characterised first by Egyptian influence (Ptolemy's), and then by Syrian (Seleucid), from which Antiochus Epiphanes rose.

It is an interesting period in that it is the story of the evil one's insidious, consistent, quiet attempts over many years to corrupt God's people, destroy their distinctiveness and frustrates God's Purpose.

The great weapon he used was "Hellenism." It was not so much a frontal attack, but from within: "Make the boat so rotten underwater that a few shots will finally sink it!" He sought to do this by Hellenising the cities, building Gentile Hellenic cities in the land as centres of Greek thought and culture, corrupting the rulers and priesthood (Hellenists—Sadducees) and compromising the spirituality of God's own including their life, service, and worship, ultimately to corrupt the royal seed of David if possible. The end purpose was to make it impossible for the Messiah to come. Thus this period is the story on one hand of worldliness, compromise, and satanic alliance; and on the other, a story of spiritual reaction and triumph (Chasidim, Pharisees, Essenes, etc.)

Some of the high priests were godly and devout men who knew the Lord including Simon the Just (Chasidim), Onias IV (Head of Pharisees) to name a few; others were evil such as Onias II who was wealthy through pocketing taxes, Jason (a great Hellenist with a Greek name who "bought" the high priesthood) and Menelaus who outbid Jason!

The struggle between these two forces—purity and compromise, heaven and earth, spirit and flesh—grew in intensity like a rumbling volcano until with the Maccabees it erupted.

The Maccabean Period

The Macccabean period extends from the rise of Antiochus Epiphanes in 175 BC to Pompey's conquest of the Promised Land in 63 BC, a period of 112 years.

We come now to the person of Antiochus Epiphanes, whose policy and character dominate this period. Antiochus Epiphanes was a remarkable personality and character. He was affable, genial, and generally liked, particularly by the more cultured. He was liked in Rome, and with the esteem and affection of Athens by his democratic ways, and by his many gifts to the city including various temples, buildings, etc., they made him an honorary citizen, and master of the mint. He was also a good soldier and an able administrator.

When he became king of Syria, as Antiochus IV, his avowed policy was to unify all the different nations and races in his kingdom through the dissemination of Greek culture and thought. He was not a foundational religionist but an enthusiastic believer in Hellenistic culture and civilization with a deep concern for the unity, social well-being and development of his kingdom.

Through Hellenism he believed that not only could the Greek Empire be unified, but also the whole of the Mediterranean and Asia area. The Jews, therefore, especially those in the land with their utter distinctiveness who were set apart in every way, when they settled amongst Gentiles were his great problem.

Indeed they completely frustrated his policy. Whilst the Jews remained true Jews, there was no hope of success. Their refusal to worship idols or even admit other Gods, their rejection of Greek philosophy, their food laws, their distinctive dress and conduct, not least their horror of intermarriage, all spelt trouble for him. Indeed, some of their objections were pure obstinacy and unreasonableness to him.

This was a challenge which Antiochus meant to answer and conquer. He was greatly encouraged by not a few Jews, those children of God who were ready to welcome his policy and cooperate with him fully. This made the others appear all the more unreasonable.

Antiochus believed not only in the worship of Greek gods, particularly Zeus (Jupiter), but also in himself as the visible manifestation of Zeus—his name *Epiphanes* meant "God manifest" (changed by wage to "Epimanes"—madman).

His plan, therefore, was to eradicate Judaism, and colonise the whole land with Hellenised people. He began by removing the godly Onias IV, replacing him with Jason, a Hellenist, who was to carry out his policy in Judea. Jason started by building a Greek gymnasium in Jerusalem and encouraging Greek dress and fashions. Many of the more Hellenised Jews began to worship Zeus as Jehovah and Jehovah as Zeus.

As Antiochus was fighting in Egypt he heard that the people in Judea went wild in rejoicing at his rumoured death. He returned suddenly in a fury, plundered Jerusalem, massacring thousands and instituted a barbaric military governor.

Shortly afterwards he began to really put his plan into effect. In 167 BC by royal decree the distinctive characteristics of God's children were to be removed. The law was publicly banned, an army of 20,000 entered Jerusalem on the Sabbath and profaned the temple. All services and sacrifices were forbidden. Nehemiah's walls were destroyed and Jerusalem was to be turned into a Greek city-state. Pagan altars were set up everywhere, and God's people had to participate in pagan rites on pain of death.

In 167 BC, also by royal decree, circumcision was forbidden as was Sabbath observance, and even the reading of the law on pain of death. The land ran with the blood of the faithful; no one was spared. Immoral orgies took place in the temple, and Jews were forced to eat pork and other unclean foods.

Towards the end of 167 BC the persecution, the most devilish attempt in the whole history of God's people to systematically destroy them, culminated in the erection over the brazen altar an altar to Jupiter with a statue. On this was offered swine's flesh. This was the "Abomination of Desolation." Moffat translates it as "appalling horror."[1] The Hebrews knew Zeus or Jupiter as Ba'al with all that that meant.

---

1 See Daniel 4:31, 12:11; Matthew 24:15

It had become impossible to live as a true child of God; the only alternatives were death or compromise. Many of the Jews compromised and went along with the measures; others passively resisted; others died in open opposition. This most terrible part of the persecution lasted about three and half years.

But the really active opposition began when an old man, a priest, godly and devout, called Mattathias, who lived not far from Jerusalem, slew both the Greek officer and an apostate Jew who was taking part in a pagan rite. He and his five sons fled to the hills with many others and began a guerrilla campaign. He died that year but his sons under the leadership of Judas Maccabeus, began systematic military campaigns with great successes.

The Maccabees that had arisen were often known by their family name of Hasmoneans. They freed Jerusalem and re-consecrated the temple. Antiochus died on a campaign in Media in 164 BC.

When Judas died in battle, his brother fortunately carried on, becoming also high priest. The objective of complete independence and freedom was won by Simon, their youngest brother, who took over when Jonathan died. It was the first time since well before the exile that God's people were truly free. In fact the Maccabees were to recover nearly all the territory that Daniel ruled, and to give us one of the most stirring eras in the history of God's children.

The Post Maccabean Period

This last short period we will consider began with Pompey's conquest of the Promised Land in 63 BC and ends with the birth of Christ in 6 BC approximately. Although short, this period is noteworthy in that it saw the people of God come under Roman law and government, the rise of the Herods, the rebuilding of the temple, the quickening anticipation of the coming Messiah, and the preparation of a tiny but faithful remnant—all this in less than sixty years.

By the end of the actual Maccabean period most of the original land of Israel had been recovered, and the Gentile Hellenising forces checked though not eliminated. Nevertheless, the close of that era was marked by decline and deterioration of spiritual life and character, by civil war, and continual internal discussion and corruption. This invited Roman interest and Pompey finally took the region for Rome in 63 BC.

The decline and deterioration continued throughout these sixty years. The forces that stood against it either became as the Pharisees, more and more formal and legalistic, or as the Essenes, who were more divorced from life and extremist.

About twenty years after the Roman conquest in 40 BC, through much intrigue and diplomacy, Herod was recognized by Augustus as King of Judea. He was a ruthless, cruel and brilliant man. Thus began the rule of the Herods. His reign was to last until the birth of Christ, and his greatest feat was the rebuilding of the temple into a building of magnificent proportions. The rest of his reign was a story of cruelty, compromise, murder and intrigue.

Thus, by the time of Christ's birth, God's people were fully under the Roman yoke, ruled by Edomite-Arab Herods. The Pharisees, who were the majority party in the Sanhedrin, wielded tremendous power amongst the people but were utterly servile to Rome. The aristocratic Sadducees were wedded to both

Hellenism and Rome. The Essenes were separatists and exclusives, but with more real spiritual life than any other group. And there were the common people who were longing for the mysterious Person of the Messiah who would restore Israel and rid them of their Gentile yoke and influence, bringing in the kingdom of God on earth.

The greatest move of all was perhaps the most silent and hidden; simply put it was God's preparation of the faithful remnant. Little did they know that all the ages hinged upon them and that their eyes would behold the ancient prophecies fulfilled. Indeed, they would be the witnesses of God made man! The very history of God's people had narrowed down to them!! There was Zecharias and Elisabeth and John (Luke 1); Joseph and Mary (Matthew 1:18); Simeon (Luke 2:25); Anna (Luke 2:36); the shepherds (Luke 2:8–9); the wise men (Matthew 2:1), and others. They were prepared, and they knew their Builder!

Indeed, they were the literal fulfilment of Malachi 3:16. They were not people with big ideas but knew the fear of the Lord and were faithful and devoted. And so the Lord would prepare in our day and generation such a remnant, faithful, devoted, looking for and waiting upon His coming.

Summary

So as we look back over these so called 400 silent years we see God at work in history preparing everything for the appearing of the Messiah. Indeed, by the time of Christ's birth there had been forged an amazing and until that time unique combination.

The Greeks gave the world their language, culture and a deep discontent with things as they were both in life and religion, along with an eager hunger for something new. Thus God, though they knew it not, unified the ancient world in language and culture from Spain to India, for Greek was understood everywhere. For the first time since Babel almost a 100,000,000 people could be reached by one tongue.

The Romans gave the world their unparalleled law and administration; a transport system unknown before; and an overall military security in an empire estimated to be about 56,800,000. Thus by Christ's coming, the world was a place of rest as it had not been for millenniums, embraced by an empire of all races and nations, free to exchange ideas within certain limits, governed by law, and defended by military might.

The Jews gave to the world the Word of God, the knowledge and experience of the living God, the revelation of God's eternal purpose, the promise and anticipation of the Messiah. Through the Hellenists there were synagogues throughout the whole Roman Empire and beyond, centres of Bible study and prayer, and fellowship through which the living God could make Himself known. They translated the Word of God into Greek; and their services heard of the promise of the coming Messiah. Numbers of Gentile converts who were tired of the depravity and corruption of the Gentile's religion were attached to these synagogues.

So we find a secure and mighty empire with a common language and culture; a common law and overall government; centres of Bible study and prayer, Greek speaking everywhere from which the truth is disseminated. We find a discontent with things as they were; an eager anticipation of a coming Messiah;

and highways along which the good news could be spread. Had there ever been such a combination of factors before? Surely it was the "fullness of time" when God sent forth His Son (Galatians 4:4).

For one quiet night a rough and simple cave used for cattle and sheep just outside a little known town among the Judean hills in the great Roman Empire became the scene of the greatest event in history. *Christ was born!*

The fact is that in spite of antichrist, the compromise of God's people, a form of godliness but the denying of the power thereof, and in spite of all the energy and cunning of Satan, even though he is the Prince of this world, Christ appears! God's purpose is fulfilled.

The last great act of this period to nullify the purpose of God was the massacre of the innocents at Christ's birth (Matthew 2:16–18), and it failed! And so it will be with us! In spite of everything CHRIST WILL APPEAR and all will be FULFILLED.

As we look back over these many years, few of us I am sure, have ever realized how much was contained in, and lies behind, the simple super-ascription nailed above Christ's head as He finished His work—*Jesus of Nazareth, The King of The Jews* written in Hebrew, Greek and Latin

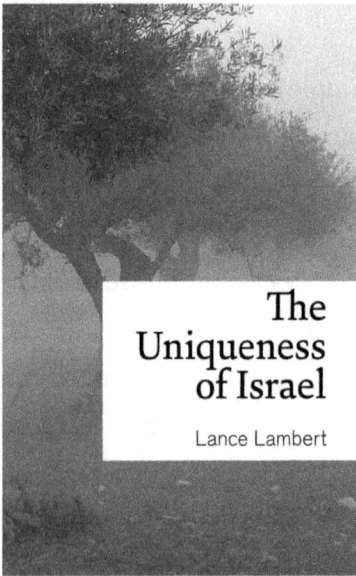

The
Uniqueness
of Israel

Lance Lambert

The Uniqueness of Israel

Woven into the fabric of Jewish existence there is an undeniable uniqueness. There is bitter controversy over the subject of Israel, but time itself will establish the truth about this nation's place in God's plan. For Lance Lambert, the Lord Jesus is the key that unlocks Jewish history He is the key not only to their fall, but also to their restoration. For in spite of the fact that they rejected Him, He has not rejected them.

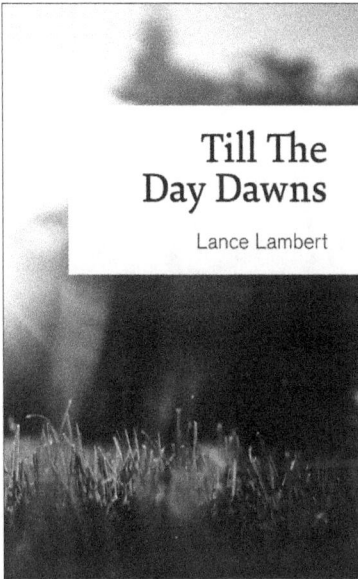

Till The
Day Dawns

Lance Lambert

Till the Day Dawns

"And we have the word of prophecy made more sure; whereunto ye do well that ye take heed, as unto a lamp shining in a dark place, until the day dawn, and the day-star arise in your hearts." (II Peter 1:9).

The word of prophecy was not given that we might merely be comforted but that we would be prepared and made ready. Let us look into the Word of God together, searching out the prophecies, that the Day-Star arise in our hearts until the Day dawns.

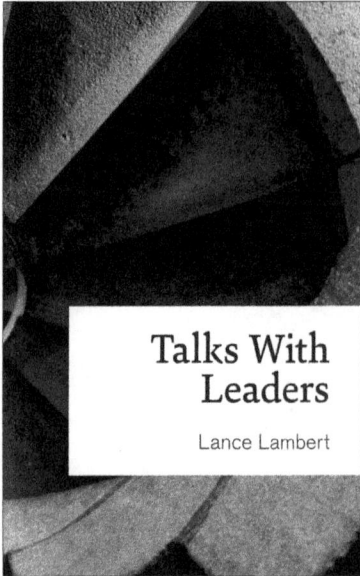

Talks With Leaders

"O Timothy, guard that which is committed unto thee ..." (1 Timothy 6:20) Has God given you something? Has God deposited something in you? Is there something of Himself which He has given to you to contribute to the people of God? Guard it. Guard that vision which He has given you. Guard that understanding that He has so mercifully granted to you. Guard that experience which He has given that it does not evaporate or drain away or become a cause of pride. Guard that which the Lord has given to you by the Holy Spirit. In these heart-to-heart talks with leaders Lance Lambert covers such topics as the character of God's servants, the way to serve, the importance of anointing, and hearing God's voice. Let us consider together how to remain faithful with what has been entrusted to us.

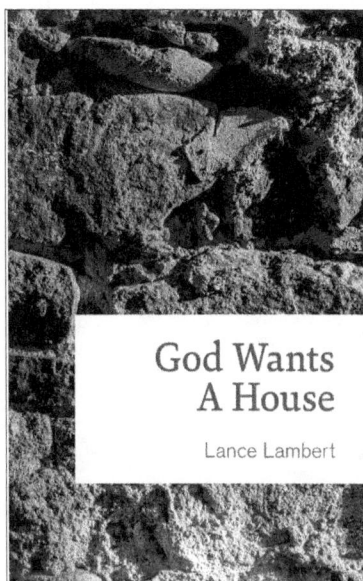

God Wants a House

Where is God at home? Is He at home in Richmond, VA? Is He at home in Washington? Is He at home in Richmond, Surrey? Is He at home in these other places? Where is God at home? There are thousands of living stones, many, many dear believers with real experience of the Lord, but where has the ark come home? Where are the staves being lengthened that God has finally come home? In God Wants a House Lance looks into this desire of the Lord, this desire He has to dwell with His people. What would this dwelling look like? Let's seek the Lord, that we can say with David, "One thing have I asked of Jehovah, that will I seek after: that I may dwell in the house of Jehovah all the days of my life, To behold the beauty of Jehovah, And to inquire in his temple."

www.ingramcontent.com/pod-product-compliance
Lightning Source LLC
Chambersburg PA
CBHW061155040426
42445CB00013B/1692